London Travel Guide for Women

For Women, by Women: The Insider's Guide to "The Old Smoke"

By Erica Stewart

© 2017 by Erica Stewart
© 2017 by ALEX-PUBLISHING
All rights reserved

Published by:

Table of Contents

Author's Note
What To Consider Before Visiting London
What Should I Know about the Currency?
When is the Best Time to Visit London?
Transportation & Lodging
What's the Best Way to Get around London?
Ideas of Where to Stay in London
Things to See and Do in London
The London Nightlife Scene
London Dining Experiences
The London Art Scene
Shopping in London
London Walking and Biking Tours
Biking in and around London
Conclusion
Helpful Resources
**** PREVIEW OTHER BOOKS BY THIS AUTHOR****

© Copyright 2015

All rights reserved. No part of this book may be reproduced or transmitted in any form or by any means, electronically or mechanically, including photocopy, recording, or by any information storage or retrieval system, without the written permission from the publisher, except in the case of brief quotations embodied in critical articles or reviews.

Trademarks are the property of their respective holders. When used, trademarks are for the benefit of the trademark owner only.

DISCLAIMER

The information provided herein is stated to be truthful and consistent, in that any liability, in terms of inattention or otherwise, by any usage or abuse of any policies, processes, or directions contained within is the solitary and utter responsibility of the recipient reader. Under no circumstances will any legal responsibility or blame be held against the publisher for any reparation, damages, or monetary loss due to the information herein, either directly or indirectly. Respective authors hold all rights not held by publisher.

Author's Note

London is the world's most popular tourist destination. It hosts over thirty million visitors annually. Whether you travel as a single woman or in the company of a group of women, travelling as female has its own set of concerns and challenges. Others who hear we are travelling alone, or with "a bunch of women", are either fearful for our safety without "men to protect us", or they feel sorry for us having to travel alone. As writer Kristin Newman points out in her book, "What I Was Doing While You Were Breeding", there is a stigma about individuals eating alone, going to the movies alone, sightseeing alone or travelling alone. This is especially so for women.

Jennifer Hoddevik, founder of Travel Yogi, whose clientele is 85% women, notes that most of her clients are travelling alone. Safety is a fair concern. But travelling alone isn't the same as being alone. There are things you can do to minimize risks and still enjoy participating in what you came to do. She states that nights are the trickiest time and suggests that women travelling alone sign up for day trips. They are safer, they are often less expensive, you see a lot more than you'd see at night, you meet interesting people with shared interests and there is an added element of safety.

Since some women prefer to join a group of women for the purposes of travel, new travel businesses like Women Traveling Together have begun to cater solely to this niche market. The business was started by a forty-year-old woman who didn't want to travel as a single on couple's tours. As you see, there are many options out there for women travelling solo or in groups.

The purpose of this book is to explore tour options in and around London. Destinations and activities are especially geared to women who want to travel alone or in the company of other women. How is this book different from your typical travelogue of London? First, the sites are ones specifically recommended as "must see" destinations by other women. Second, the tips offered are provided especially for women travelers. Lastly, realistically, there are places, which would be uncomfortable, if not downright dangerous, for women to visit. These are red flagged as a courtesy to our fellow women travelers.

In this book, you will find invaluable tips for women. For instance, never pass by a free loo. Most pubs, restaurants, and museums have free use loos. But, always carry at least 40 pence for the ladies' room. In many public places in London, you have to pay to use the loo. Prices vary from 20 pence to 40 pence. The most common price is 30 pence. Be prepared. Now as a woman, don't you think this is a valuable piece of travel information?

London is an exciting city full of all sorts of interesting and educational destinations for women. We'll discuss many of them as well as easy and inexpensive ways to see London.

    Erica Stewart

Author's Note
What To Consider Before Visiting London
    What Should I Know about the Currency?
    When is the Best Time to Visit London?
Transportation & Lodging
    What's the Best Way to Get around London?
    Ideas of Where to Stay in London
Things to See and Do in London
    The London Nightlife Scene
    London Dining Experiences
    The London Art Scene
    Shopping in London
    London Walking and Biking Tours
    Biking in and around London

Conclusion
    Helpful Resources
**** PREVIEW OTHER BOOKS BY THIS AUTHOR****
  "FLORENCE FOR WOMEN: THE ULTIMATE TRAVEL GUIDE FOR WOMEN"

What To Consider Before Visiting London

If you're from an English-speaking country, you don't need a visa and you can stay up to six months. All you need is a passport with an expiration date later than the date of your return to the USA. When you are getting ready to travel, be sure to check the latest regulations. Most countries are becoming stricter about passports. Make sure yours is current.

What Should I Know about the Currency?

Unlike most of Europe, England has not adopted the Euro. They use pounds sterling. As well, if you plan to use credit or debit cards visit your bank before you leave. Otherwise you may find your card denied.

When is the Best Time to Visit London?

The best answer to this question is: That all depends. London has many things to offer the traveler. What you can do and see depends on the time of year.

January in London is a shoppers' bonanza. It is low tourist season so a good time to be here and capture accommodations and travel bargains. Bundle up, bring your skates, and come shop the post-Christmas sales. There are lots of free outdoor activities in January in the city as well.

Enjoy the New Year's Day parade with its floats and brass bands. January is also the time for the London Boat Show, which showcases hundreds of water vessels of every shape and size. If you enjoy a surreal experience then come and be a part of the London International Mime Festival. It is a celebration of visual theatre featuring the world's best mime artists and companies.

February in London offers romance and comfort. It's still a low tourist season so take advantage of smaller crowds, less expensive hotel and flight prices. Sample the legendary London eateries fare. Tuck into a quiet British pub. Take time to enjoy the Chinese traditions so evident in London in February. Chinese New Year celebrations in London are the largest outside Asia. Join London's Chinese community in the West End for a parade and other festivities. Have Chinese delicacies at one of the many Chinese restaurants in London's Chinatown. Celebrate Shrove Tuesday with Londoners by having pancakes at one of the many restaurants celebrating this beginning of the Lenten season. One of the biggest February deals in London is London Fashion Week. Enjoy makeovers, designer shopping and catwalk shows from top clothing brands at Somerset House.

March is a favorite tourist time in London. Enjoy the spring flowers. Go for walks in the warming weather as London comes alive. Watch the sporting events on the river Thames. Two major sporting events are the Head of the River Race and the Oxford and Cambridge Boat Race. Crews and spectators from around the world descend on London for these events, which are free to watch. March marks St. Patrick's Day in London. Celebrations include a parade through central London and a festival in Trafalgar Square. Traditional Irish foods are served. Dancing and Irish music celebrations are offered at many pubs and bars around the capital.

In April, London is in full bloom. Come and enjoy such free and world-famous events as the London Marathon and Oxford and Cambridge Boat Race. Now that the weather has warmed, April is a good time to get out and enjoy activities in London Parks and a cruise up the Thames. It is also a good time to explore London Wetland Centre in Southwest London. Don't forget to check out the ducklings and new chicks. Take part in the free St George's Day celebrations in Trafalgar Square. St George, the patron saint of England, is famous for slaying a dragon. Festivities in his honour include food, parades and children's activities.

May marks the beginning of all sorts of open-air events as the weather warms up. Look for pop up eateries, clubs, flower shows, exciting cultural celebrations and fun activities for all ages. In May attend the Chelsea Flower Show or tour the innovative show gardens. Hotels and restaurants hold special afternoon teas and have special menus for this world-famous show. May outdoor events include festivals in London's many parks. Regent's Park Open Air Theatre opens its season in its beautiful outdoor amphitheatre. It's a good time for visitors to enjoy London's many live theatre offerings. Check out the street food and Brewster festivals. Favourites include: Kerb's Alchemy. Kerb's spiciest street food superstars move into the Southbank Centre's marketplace for eleven days in May for the Alchemy festival. They offer dishes from Pakistan, Nepal, Sri Lanka and Afghanistan. This year marks the fourth festival of craft beer in Greenwich. Crowds gather at The Old Brewery in The Royal Naval College for three days of beer tasting, food pairing and live music.

June is the month for celebrating such events as the Queen's birthday parade, Trooping the Colour, and tennis at Wimbledon. If you are a foodie, don't miss the whirlwind tour of London's restaurant scene at the Taste of London festival. London's top chefs and restaurants serve delectable menus and hold cooking demonstrations in Regent's Park. June is also the time for London's premier polo event. Attend polo weekend at Chesterton Humberts Polo in the Park. Women take note: this event comes with food, champagne and luxury shopping.

July when it is hot in many places is just comfortable in London. It's a good month to be in the capital city for shopping, walking tours, outdoor activities and cultural celebrations. It is also time to enjoy rock, pop or dance music at one of London's music festivals. Events are held in parks, such as Lovebox in Victoria Park and Queen Elizabeth Olympic Park. This is the month when Buckingham Palace opens giving visitors a chance to tour and the world-famous Hampton Court Palace Flower Show attracts visitors from around the world.

August in London offers tourists Europe's biggest street party. Notting Hill Carnival in West London showcases West Indian culture. The carnival includes two days of floats, parades, music and dance for the over a million people who attend. There are lots of child-friendly attractions if you are travelling with children on summer vacation.

In September, the city fairly pulses with festivals and free city-wide celebrations. There are many things taking place on the river. One example is the Great River Race. Over 300 vessels cross a twenty-one-mile route past some of London's most iconic landmarks plying oars and paddles. September's London Design Festival presents exhibitions, educational seminars, lectures, installations, and parties at various locations throughout the city. The Pearly Kings and Queens Harvest Festival honours harvest season with a spectacular parade through the city.

October is food and drink season. Take a tour of London parks to enjoy the fall colours. Kids are on break this month so many locations including: Science Museum,

Natural History Museum, the Tower of London and Southbank Centre have special events and programs for them. Much is made of Halloween here with costumes, haunted houses, parties and trick or treating. October is [London Restaurant Festival](#)'s month-long celebration of London's top restaurants and celebrity chefs. Enjoy the special one-off menus and food-themed events. Art lovers will want to be in London in October for the Frieze Art Fair festival at Regent's Park. This includes contemporary art stalls, exhibitions and talks.

If you like the weather a bit nippier, London in November is a great time to sightsee before Christmas crowds descend. It's also a good time to visit the city's cosy little pubs. November highlights include the Lord Mayor's Show. This is an eight-hundred-year inauguration ceremony including a huge procession of marching bands, floats, and acrobats as well as an evening fireworks display. November activities abound with fireworks as Guy Fawkes or Bonfire Night is held on November fifth with much fanfare and fireworks. November is also London's celebration of London Jazz Festival. The show pays tribute to musical talent and jazz stars.

If you love Christmas crowds, Christmas shopping and spectacular Christmas extravaganzas like the famous fireworks at the London Eye, pop-up ice rinks and incredible New Year's Eve celebrations, then bundle up and come to London for the Christmas season. In Trafalgar Square, the city's biggest Christmas tree welcomes locals and out-of-towners to join in carol sings all over London. Carol services are held on the square throughout the month. Local clubs, restaurants and pubs consider December an invitation to hold special events. December is one long party in London.

No matter when you visit London there is always something exciting to see and do. Strap on a pair of skates and join the crowd at one of the many pop up ice rinks like those at Somerset House and the Natural History Museum.

Whether you are travelling as a single woman, as part of a group, or you have your kids with you, there is no end to the activities London offers at any time of the year.

Transportation & Lodging

What's the Best Way to Get around London?

Travelling alone or as part of a group you will probably want to use one of the infamous black cabs of London or the gleaming crimson double decker buses. If you are staying for more than three or four days, invest in an Oyster Card. This makes travel a good deal cheaper and easier. Just swipe it to board any bus or the Tube. Without an Oyster Card you will have to pay cash each time you board a bus or the subway. You can purchase an Oyster Card and a Tube map before you depart online by visiting the Transport for London website (https://tfl.gov.uk/). You can get one at Heathrow, Paddington Station, or at any Tube station.

If you plan to do day trips to cities outside London, there is a good train system. The trains are plentiful and user friendly. I highly recommend a train ride to Bath or Glasgow to see the English countryside.

Ideas of Where to Stay in London

London is a large city with many options for women travelling solo or as part of a large group. When it comes to accommodations, most men want convenience. They want a hotel with maid service and a restaurant, if not in the hotel, then nearby. They want transportation options that are handy and easy to access.

Women travelers are usually more adventurous. They enjoy some place that has the comforts of home like a boutique hotel, an apartment or a bed and breakfast. They are often perfectly fine with doing a little light housekeeping and fixing breakfast or even lunch themselves.
You can choose from B&B rooms to centrally located hotels, condos and apartments in London. If you want to experience English countryside hospitality you may wish to consider a country home hotel.
Try a cozy two-bedroom two-bath apartment whether you are staying for a night or a fortnight. This one is located in quaint Greenwich Village. Take your choice of any one of three apartments. Each sleeps six and includes both cooking and laundry facilities, central heating/cooling and Internet access. The apartments are wheelchair accessible and pet and smoker friendly. Available through http://www.tripadvisor.com/VRACSearch?geo=186338&nuid=BA0069D636C49703E4C6A58A08361308&l1currency=USD&firstVRs=1652715&token=8a9076d73ca4553763afa434101cd216 these units book months ahead and start at $203/night.

If you are not travelling with a big group then this one bedroom, one bath priced at $186 may fit your needs. It sleeps up to four people. The attractive popular flat is located in central London in the financial district. Read the reviews and find out more about this conveniently located flat at: http://www.tripadvisor.com/VacationRentalReview-g186338-d5858199-City_of_London_1_bedroom-London_England.html.

How about a condo that sleeps six and has two baths? This one, priced just over $300/night, is in a luxurious condo built around a tropical style atrium. It's a two-minute walk to St. Paul's Cathedral, Millennium Bridge and Tate art gallery. It is also in the midst of coffee shops and pubs, restaurants and the City of London theatre district. Find out more about it at: http://www.tripadvisor.com/VacationRentalReview-g186338-d8151540-SUPERIOR_2_BEDROOM_APT_ST_PAUL_s_Zone1_WiFi-London_England.html.

If it's a picturesque, old hotel that strikes your fancy, then the Hilton London Euston is conveniently situated in the Bloomsbury district in the heart of the capital. The building is stunningly restored Victorian architecture. Book over a week ahead and you can save up to 20%. It's a short walk to the Tube and Euston. The hotel boasts a delicious breakfast, accommodating staff and quiet rooms. http://www3.hilton.com/en/hotels/united-kingdom/hilton-london-euston-LONEUHI/index.html

Photo courtesy of Hilton London Euston Hotel

Ambassadors Bloomsbury is located in the same section of London. It is known for comfortably sized, clean rooms with good amenities like Wi-Fi, a flat screen TV, a Nespresso machine, and quiet rooms, at a very good price. The hotel is well located within walking distance of The British Museum, British Library, the Harry Potter tour, and King's Cross Station. http://www.ambassadors.co.uk/welcome-homehtml.

Photo courtesy of Ambassador Bloomsbury

If you want something roomier in a hotel location, The Wesleyan in Camden is a good choice. You can book a single, a double or a triple at this clean modern hotel. Staff members are very welcoming and friendly and the continental breakfast is nothing short of amazing. The hotel is located in a quiet Regent Park neighbourhood within walking distance to bus stops and the Tube. Good price, modern conveniences, and friendly staff all combine to make this a great location for sightseeing trips. http://www.thewesley.co.uk/.

Photo courtesy The Wesleyan, Camden

Perhaps a bed and breakfast is more your cup of tea? Then check out The Cleveland hotel/B&B, located in picturesque Bayswater. It has clean spacious rooms with comfortable beds. The Cleveland is conveniently located near the underground, near Kensington Park, and Kensington Palace.

Rhodes Avenue Homestay B&B is conveniently located if you fly into Heathrow. Simply board the Tube and remain on the Piccadilly Line to Bounds Green. There are three buses that pass near the station and go down the street toward Rhodes Avenue, and all run at short intervals, so there is little waiting time. Buses into Central London and the Piccadilly Line Tube make transit a snap. Use your Oyster card to get around London easily. From this quiet location you can do the tourist thing almost as easily as staying in Central London, and you avoid the crush of tourists. http://www.rhodesavenue.com/#Home. The hearty breakfast will keep you going all day. Find out more at: http://www.tripadvisor.ca/Hotel_Review-g186338-d3296471-Reviews-Rhodes_Avenue_Homestay_B_B-London_England.html.

Photo courtesy of oyster.com

Located in scenic Dulwich, The Lilac Door is the perfect accommodation for those who enjoy B&B as opposed to a hotel. Guests rave about The Maitresse's hospitality as well as her biscuits and coffee. The Lilac Door is located in a lovely part of South London, convenient for the sights but far from the crowds. Find out more at: http://www.lilacdoor.co.uk/.

Photo courtesy of Pinterest

Why not consider accommodations at a traditional English countryside spot near London? The traditional English country house is unique. This post-war concept became popular amongst city workers looking for rest and relaxation. Private homes were converted into hotels. These specialised in offering guests cozy personal accommodations. There are around 5,000 traditional English country accommodations.

Locate just thirty miles outside London; in east Sussex, Gravetye Manor is one of Britain's greatest, and longest-living, country house hotels. Elegant new furnishings make this seventeen-bedroom estate look elegant, fresh and attractive. Each bedroom has its own bath. http://www.gravetyemanor.co.uk/.

If you are a Thomas Hardy fan and you'd like to stay in a quaint village, then Summer Lodge on the edge of Evershot is just the Dorset-area vacation spot for you. Owner Beatrice Tollman has lent her special touch of feminine and the flouncy to this estate with its fabric covered ceilings and padded fabric walls. The drawing room was designed by Thomas Hardy. Bedrooms are divinely pretty and comfortable for any female traveller. http://www.summerlodgehotel.co.uk/.

Photo courtesy of Summer Lodge, Dorset

Hambleton Hall in Rutland is a late Victorian house. Since 1978, it has overlooked Rutland Water in a most beautiful and evocative landscape. The house exudes class and money. The sumptuous country house is surrounded by lovely English gardens that offer an intrinsic view of Rutland Water from the charming flower-filled terrace.

Meals are prepared by the famous chef, Aaron Patterson, who trained here as a 16-year-old sous chef.
http://www.hambletonhall.com/

Photo courtesy of Hambleton Hall

From posh downtown hotels to convenient apartments, B&Bs, and country home accommodations, London has something that is just perfect for every woman, whether she is travelling alone or is part of a large or small group.

Things to See and Do in London

Even if you are not a thrill rider, The London Eye will be worth it just for the photo op. You'll find this massive Ferris wheel on the Thames River's South Bank in the borough of Lambeth. Also it is known as the Millennium Wheel, the London Eye has been rebranded as the Coca Cola London Eye since January. It has been called Europe's tallest Ferris wheel; it stands 443 feet tall. The diameter of the wheel measures 394 feet. Built in 1999, it was then the tallest of the Ferris wheels of the world. Its operators call it "the world's tallest cantilevered observation wheel". The view from the top is worth the cost of the ride. https://www.londoneye.com/

Discover a thousand years of British history at The Tower of London, located in central London on the North Bank of the Thames. The castle belongs to her Majesty and lies within the Tower Hamlets borough of London. It sits just outside the city proper on an open space called Tower Hill. Built in 1066 as part of the Norman Conquest by William the Conqueror. It was viewed by British as a symbol of Norman oppression. From 1100 to 1952 it was used as a prison. But in its heyday it was a grand palace and an early a royal residence. The Tower is actually a complex of several buildings within two concentric rings. These walls and the moat were built for defense. The Tower of London was expanded under Richard the Lionheart, Henry III, and Edward I. But after the 13th century the tower remained unchanged.

http://www.hrp.org.uk/TowerOfLondon/

Photo courtesy of The Tower of London

While you're there be sure to see The Crown Jewels. Part of the Royal collection the Crown Jewels include world famous diamonds still used by Queen Elizabeth II. Walk the Tower walls, which have protected kings and queens since Henry III's thirteenth century fortifications. Explore the Medieval Palace and the seven huge towers: the Salt, Broad Arrow, Constable, Martin, 'Royal Beasts', Bowyer and Flint Tower.

If you are planning on learning more about the history of Great Britain, a good place to start is the British Museum. The following buses stop at Oxford Street: 1, 7, 8, 19, 25, 38, 55, 98, 242. In addition Holborn, Tottenham, Russell Square and Goodge Street underground stops are nearby.

Highlights include a wealth of exhibits of various eras. You could spend an entire day on the Egyptian exhibit alone. Be sure to take one of the guided tours first and then go back and see specific areas of interest afterward. There is so much to see here you will want to allow at least a day to tour this outstanding museum. Admission is free although there is a cost for tours. http://www.britishmuseum.org/

Everyone who goes to London visits Buckingham Palace, the official residence of Queen Elizabeth II. Buckingham Palace receives fifteen million visitors a year. Once a large townhouse, it was built for the Duke of Buckingham. It was later acquired by King George III as a private residence for Queen Charlotte and called "The Queen's House". In the 1800's it was enlarged, adding three wings around a central courtyard. Queen Victoria made it the official residence in 1837. Tour the building and see works of art from the Royal Collection.

Buckingham Palace is open to visitors just eight weeks each year. Walk in the footsteps of kings and queens. Take an audio tour or sign up for the official tour of the royal residence. The official tour (over $100 Canadian dollars for adults) takes you through staterooms and up the Grand staircase. A favourite destination is the Throne Room. You will also see the Ballroom. A

http://www.royal.gov.uk/theroyalresidences/buckingh ampalace/buckinghampalace.aspx

Be sure to stay for the Changing of the Guard. It occurs at 11:30 each morning. Times are posted on the official website at: http://www.changing-the-guard.com/dates-times.html

Another not-to-be missed location is the National Gallery –London. Here you will see works by such famous artists as: Botticelli, Rembrandt, Gainsborough, Leonardo da Vinci, Turner, Renoir and Van Gogh. The gallery has over 2,000 paintings from Western Europe alone, and dating from the middle ages to the twentieth century. Admission is free. While you are there check out the special exhibitions, video, art lectures, and audio-visual programmes. You can take one of the guided tours and there are special holiday events for both children and adults. http://www.nationalgallery.org.uk/

Remember when you were a child and sang, "London Bridge is Falling down"? Well you can't see that bridge unless you go to Arizona, but you can see the equally interesting Tower Bridge. Built from 1886 until 1894, the Tower Bridge is a combined bascule and suspension bridge in London. It crosses the Thames right near the Tower of London. It is one of five London bridges. The Tower Bridge connects the City of London to the Southwark bank. http://www.towerbridge.org.uk/

If you have a friend of a friend or a distant relative who is a member of the London Ladies Club don't miss an opportunity to go. Begun in 1994, the London Ladies Club provides members and guests a place to meet and talk. The club meets Tuesday morning at The Army and Navy Club in Pall Mall. Membership is open to ladies of all ages and social classes. Information about the talks is posted three times a year in the club Newsletter, *London Lady,* and on their website.

Big Ben is official clock of the houses of Parliament building. Don't miss it! The hands are 4.2 metres long and weigh 100 kg. At first, the clock wouldn't work because the hands were too heavy. Big Ben's time is strictly regulated by a pile of coins on the pendulum. The clock has rarely stopped since it first rang out the hours in 1863. Even the bombings of London did not stop Big Ben. While you're there take a tour of the Parliament buildings. http://www.parliament.uk/bigben.

The M16 Building is a favourite of the ladies. Also known as the SIS Building, this structure houses Great Britain's Secret Intelligence Service (SIS), also known as MI6. The building is located at 85 Albert Embankment in Vauxhall, in the southwestern area of central London. It was built on the banks of the Thames River near Vauxhall Bridge.

While you are in London, take a history tour of contemporary and historical figures at Madame Tussaud's Wax Museum. Stars of film, Bollywood, Sports, Cultural heroes, and the Royal Family are captured for posterity. You will meet musical icons, world leaders and get your blood racing in the popular but hair-raising chamber of horrors. Experience a virtual tour of London aboard one of London's infamous black cabs and enjoy Star Wars and 4-D movies. For more information and to preplan your trip, click on: https://www.madametussauds.com/London/

Saint Paul's Cathedral is worth the visit for the architecture alone. The Anglican cathedral, the seat of the Bishop of London, is located on Ludgate Hill. The view from this highest point of the City of London is spectacular. Take some time to tour the church, a work of famed architect Sir Christopher Wren. For more information about visit times, guided tours, and church service times, click on: https://www.stpauls.co.uk/

Founded in 960, Westminster Abbey is a mainly Gothic architecture. Its formal name is the Collegiate Church of St Peter at Westminster located near the Palace of Westminster. One of the most visited London sites; it is home to kings, queens, statesmen and soldiers, poets, priests, heroes and villains. It is little wonder that this icon welcomes over a million visitors to explore this seven-hundred-year-old building. Westminster Abbey is a working chapel that has daily services. Audio self-guided tours are available in several languages. The guided verger-led tours are very popular. For hours, tours, and service times click on: http://www.westminster-abbey.org/visit-us/opening-times.

Trafalgar Square, named to commemorate the Battle of Trafalgar, is a public space in central London, in the area formerly known as Charing Cross. Like Westminster Abbey, Trafalgar Square is situated in the City of Westminster. Nelson's Column, located in the centre of the square, is guarded by four lion statues at the column's base. Several commemorative statues and sculptures fill the square. The square has been the site of political demonstrations, community gatherings, and the New Year's Eve celebrations.

Piccadilly Circus, located in London's West End, is not a circus at all. It is actually a road junction with the City of Westminster. It was built in 1819 to connect Regent Street with Piccadilly. Circus, in this context, is derived from the Latin *circus*, meaning, "circle". Piccadilly Circus is a round open space at a street junction. It is an excellent photo opportunity and a chance to tell the folks back home you were there! The location has become somewhat of a circus, because Piccadilly now links directly to the theatres on Shaftesbury Avenue, the Haymarket, Coventry Street near Leicester Square, and Glasshouse Street. It is close to major shopping and entertainment areas in the West End. Because it is a major traffic junction, Piccadilly Circus has become a busy meeting place. It is a famous tourist attraction, known for its video display and neon signs on the corner building, and the Shaftesbury memorial fountain and statue of Eros. The Piccadilly Tube station is located under a plaza, which houses London Pavilion, Criterion Restaurant and Criterion Theatre. Piccadilly Circus is a great place to people watch.

The London Nightlife Scene

If you are into London night life then there is no end to your choices from London Clubs to festivals to summer pop ups. Remember, London at night is a whole different scene. Travelling in groups, and taking public or private transportation that drops you off at the door and picks you up there, is recommended.

Here are some of London's hottest clubs:

Fabric
For the past sixteen years of its operation, Fabric has established a reputation as one of London's top clubs. But it is not for the faint of heart or body. We're talking hard core full out fun here. They have consistently high quality programming showcasing UK's varied strands of electronic music underground. Fabric is located in a former meatpacking warehouse. The club's three rooms feature weekend sounds with the finest low frequencies and the deepest grooves. The crowd is hip and actively on the dance floor. While Friday and Saturday nights are all about the music, Sunday night holds its own appeal with groups like WetYourSelf which fires up at eleven every Sunday Evening with deep house, funky techno, cosmic disco and Italo grooves. They play until eight on Monday morning! Fabric is the spot for those of you

who want to experience London's rich underbelly of nightlife. Check out: http://www.fabriclondon.com/ to see what's playing.

Electric Brixton
Voted one of South London's best dance venues by the clubbing crowd, Electric Brixton opened September 2011 after the owners spent a million pounds on renovations and installing a new sound system. The designers managed to maintain many of the club's original and appealing features. The club is famous for its regular drum'n'bass, electronica and dance nights, plus big name DJs and live acts. Check out the special events at: http://www.visitlondon.com/things-to-do/place/169190-electric-brixton

Heaven
If you are a serious party person, Heaven is well named for its three floors of party space, a great sound system, and a crazy lighting system in the main room. Appealing events include: cheap student nights; G-A-Y's Porn Idol and Camp Attack; and the flagship Heaven Saturdays gay night. Heaven also has regular live music events which you can check under The Arches, Villiers Street location or by clicking on: http://www.heavennightclub-london.com/

KOKO

Not to be confused with XOYO, KOKO is Camden's High Street multi-layered nightclub. KOKO has a very full events calendar. Its offerings include: live music including the popular Guilty Pleasures, Buttoned Down Disco, and Club NME, as well as DJ-led events. KOKO caters to a wide range of musical tastes ranging from rock and pop to blues and dance music. Check this month's events at: http://www.koko.uk.com/

Ministry of Sound

Ministry of Sound Superclub has been entertaining avid club-goers for two decades at its Gaunt Street location. Its four bars, four dance floors and five distinctive rooms draws big name entertainers like: Paul Oakenfold, Judge Jules and Tall Pall. You can book a room for a special event party. You can also book tickets in advance to avoid disappointment. Get there early to avoid those long queues! Check out what is playing at: http://www.ministryofsound.com/club#HM3XZybpIBH Eof6l.97. This club voted #1 dance spot on more than one occasion is a must see if you are into the club scene.

XOYO

This Shoreditch Cowper Street venue was established in 2010. XOYO quickly established a reputation as a prominent on-point clubbing space. This two-room nightclub, art space and upstairs cafe bar is close to the Old Street roundabout. X0Y0 is famous for cutting edge entertainment. Scores of London's hippest punters and party-lovers flock to XOYO each weekend to hear the latest DJs, and producers. On weekdays you can hear emerging bands and singer-songwriters. XOYO's two floors of club space afford opportunities to hear such groups as: Eats Everything, Jackmaster, The 2 Bears, Erol Alkan, Felix Da Housecat, Jacques Lu Cont, Simian Mobile Disco, Tiga, Ms Dynamite, 2ManyDJs, Digitalism, Tensnake, Mylo, Alex Metric, and Mark Ronson. Disco. B. Traits has a Thursday night residency. Find out who is playing at XOYO by clicking on http://www.xoyo.co.uk/.

Cargo
Cargo is a cool location right under railway arches. The club showcases a wide range of music. Unlike some clubs, Cargo crowds are a warm and friendly crowd. It's worth the trip to **Cargo** just for the tasty global street food canteen! If you arrive before ten Friday nights there is no cover charge. Cargo is located on Rivington Street in Shoreditch. Learn more about what's playing there by clicking on: http://www.cargo-london.com/

Corsica Studios

This light, airy club is a favourite hangout of artists and students. The atmosphere is friendly. Corsica Studios—as the name suggests—is an arts and entertainment club. Located in South London, the club has two rooms of music and a bar. For those who enjoy dubstep and garage, Corsica Studio located on Elephant Road, with its exciting, new, experimental sounds, is the place to go. To find out what is currently playing, click on http://www.corsicastudios.com/

Studio 338
Studio 338 is famous for the summer parties on its open-air terrace. When the weather gets colder, enjoy Studio 338's heated terrace or move inside the club where there is plenty of room. Studio 338's spacious property hosts some of London's top DJs including: Sankeys, Krankbrother, Hospitality and Secretsundaze. Studio 338's 338 Boord Street North Greenwich location is just a short walk from The O2. Check out what is playing by clicking on: http://studio338.co.uk/

Egg London
This Stylish full-on warehouse venue is spread across three intimate floors. You'll think of an Ibiza club when you first encounter Egg London. The outdoor courtyard is a memorable spot to cool off, chill out, or sip a cocktail under the starry skies. Known for its Sunday morning breakfast session, Egg London is a great spot

for Sunday Brunch or late Saturday dancing. Located at 200 York Way, Egg London has a twenty-four-hour license for continuous dance parties. Check out the events at: http://www.egglondon.co.uk/

Live Theatre London

Next to New York City, London's theatre district holds its own. While you're touring London don't miss a chance to see some of these world acclaimed live theatre productions along with a friend or as a group of women. For tickets, theatre locations and special offers click on: http://www.timeout.com/london/tickets-offers

Kinky Boots

This Broadway hit musical by Cyndi Lauper and Harvey Fierstein Is set in a Northampton shoe factory. It arrives fresh from New York City at London's West End Adelphi Theatre in Charing Cross this September.

The long-awaited play is based on the 2005 film. It's a true story of a shoe factory inherited by Charlie, who is committed to continuing his father's legacy. Fortunately for Charlie and his father's faltering shoe business, the shrewd entrepreneur discovers a niche market for sturdy stilettos. Charlie's life and his business rapidly change.

Pop star Cyndi Lauper wrote the music and lyrics, which won a 2013 Tony award and a 2014 Grammy award. The songs are both feel good and singable. If you see only one show while you're in London, don't miss "Kinky Boots". You'll leave the theatre humming the memorable tunes!

Wicked

For theatre goers, the Twilight werewolves, vampires hold no appeal compared to the witches of Wicked. Now in its sixth year at the Apollo Victoria, the Oz prequel "Wicked" shows no signs of waning popularity for Londoners and tourists alike. This bombastic musical with a somewhat ragtag score and a magnetic leading lady, Rachel Tucker, who plays the Wicked Witch of the West, is as enchanting in its own right as "The Wizard of Oz".

The Book of Mormon

Still the funniest show in town, "The Book of Mormon" is the brainchild of South Park creators, Trey Parker and Matt Stone. The occasional use of 'fuck' and 'cunt' and jokes about baby rape does not put this play on the list of shows to take your kids to. Aside from the language, "The Book of Mormon" plays big-hearted, note-perfect homage tribute to Broadway's golden age. It is the best West End theatre since "Matilda".

Fake it til You Make it

Opening in September at London's SoHo Theatre, "Fake It 'til You Make it" doesn't beat about the bush. The show's topic is clinical depression. The story is seen through the eyes of Tim Grayburn, and largely told in his own words using recorded conversations. There is a genuine affection between the leading lady and man. Grayburn became depressed in his mid-twenties. Unable to cope, he seeks medication and is too ashamed to talk about his condition. Then he meets Kimmings, the leading lady. 'Fake It 'til You Make It' is an honest conversation about depression and its effects on their relationship. Kimmings visual flair elevates it, illustrating the simple tale with memorable, semi-abstract set pieces, quirky dances, self-mocking humour and epic costume changes that would impress even Lady Gaga.

Matilda

Don't miss The Royal Shakespeare Company's production of "Matilda". Start practising your chalk-levitating skills. You'll find yourself face-to-face with the terrible Miss Trunchbull! Only those who have met the beast head on can truly describe that terror and telekinesis seems to be her only weakness! Luckily for you, Matilda seems to have that side of things pretty much down. The fantastic "Matilda The Musical" is playing at The Cambridge Theatre. This show played to rave reviews at Stratford-on-Avon before arriving in London's West End. An Olivier Award winner, Kelly and Minchin's musical is adapted from Roald Dahl's 1988 novel.

Jersey Boys
Playing at the Piccadilly Theatre in SoHo, Jersey Boys is the semi-biographical story of Frankie Valli and the Four Seasons' rise to fame. The show is enhanced by wonderful renditions of Bob Gaudio-penned songs. Extended song and dance routines never get in the way of a playful, incident-packed story. Jersey Boys is one of the best shows in town and an object lesson in how the jukebox musical sub-genre can spawn a genuine classic hit show. For its musical pop culture value and its history it is doubly worthwhile.

Sinatra: The Man and His Music
This tribute to Frank Sinatra is playing at SoHo's Palladium Theatre. Frank Sinatra would have been a century old this year. In this tribute, a full orchestra and a troupe of talented dancers and singers pay homage to "Old Blue Eyes". They are backed by old movie and television footage. The show, fully endorsed by the Sinatra family, is a lovely romp through Sinatra hits.

The Sting

Wilton's lovely old Victorian Music Hall presents an adaptation of the 1973 hit film "Butch Cassidy and the Sundance Kid". In case you've forgotten, that's the depression-era gangster tale that made Robert Redford and Paul Newman a famous pair and showcased the music of Scott Joplin.

Nell Gwynn

Performed outdoors at The Globe Theatre, "Nell Gwynn" is the story of Charles II's theatrical charmer and mistress, Nell Gwynn. The play describes the life of the Restoration actress, taking her from her time as an orange seller to starring onstage. It shows Nell as the King's escort. "Nell Gwynn" is a memorable tale of seventeenth century English theatre.

Jane Eyre

This Charlotte Bronte classic opens in September at National Theatre South Bank. Once staged in two separate parts, with a running time of four and a half hours, Jane Eyre is a single performance, with an outstanding cast and dynamic, music-infused story of Jane Eyre, who loves Mr. Rochester—and discovers some odd secrets in his attic.

Songs from Far Away

Playing at Young Vic in Southwark, it's an enviable twosome. British playwright Simon Stephens teams up with avant-garde director Ivo van Hove on this new project. Stephens' play is about a brother who returns home to Amsterdam following the death of his brother and tries to reconnect with him through a series of letters.

Thoroughly Modern Millie

Playing at the Landor Theatre in Stockwell, this 1973 Julie Andrews' hit has been reinvented with a lovely jazzy theme. Matthew Iliffe production of the roaring '20s has sleek hair bobs, exuberant steps and swinging flapper dresses—everything that made the twenties unique. The staging, dancing and costumes are enough to make you want to leap to your jazzy feet and do the Charleston. Light on plot, the show is a wonderful period piece.

Photograph 51

Playing at the Noel Coward Theatre in Covent Gardens, "Photograph 51" stars Hollywood mega-actress Nicole Kidman. She returns to the West End after a seventeen-year hiatus. Directed by the great Michael Grandage, Kidman stars in the UK premiere of Anna Ziegler's play 'Photograph 51'. The play is about the 1920's English scientist, Rosalind Franklin, played by Kidman. Franklin is the woman who cracked the secret of DNA.

Tipping Velvet

A brand new adaptation of Sarah Waters' hit historical novel 'Tipping the Velvet' opens in September at the Lyric Hammersmith's newly renovated theatre. Adapted by Laura Wade, the "Tipping Velvet" tells of Nancy Astley and her love affair with male impersonator Kitty Butler in 1887 and their journey to London.

London Dining Experiences

The days when people the world over criticized and mocked London's culinary skills is long past now. London is now home to many of the world's most creative and famous chefs. London restaurants have something for every tastes and budgets.

Some interesting food facts about London dining; Brits have been drinking tea for two hundred years. They neither like nor know how to make coffee. Most of them drink their tea with milk.

Fish and chips were invented in London. They are convinced they do it best—whether served in a restaurant, as pub food, or as a take-away (That's take out for the rest of us). Chips aren't chips but French fries. If you order fish and chips to go (i.e., take away) they will wrap it in newspaper.

The following restaurants have drawn the interest of food lovers.

The Wolseley on Piccadilly between Mayfair and St. James never disappoints. By its own description, this busy restaurant is "a café in the Grand European tradition". It is located in a former car showroom and decorated in art deco style. The Wolseley specializes in generous breakfasts, business lunches, or taking friend or family out for a special occasion. For more details call 020 7499 6996, or click on www.thewolseley.com.

When you think London, Icelandic food is certainly not what comes to mind. But this spot located on Portman Street in London's West End will have you rethinking whatever your preconception of Icelandic cuisine. Texture, opened in 2007, won a Michelin star in 2010. Texture includes fresh ingredients, both British and Icelandic menu items, with lots of fish and herbs. Texture's co-owner Rousset, also the restaurant's sommelier, has ensured there is an extensive wine list. Two-course lunch menus are £19.90. Three courses are available for £24.90. Tasting menus may be purchased for £79 per person. For more information and to see menus, call 020 7224 0028, or click on: www.texture-restaurant.co.uk

Galvin at Windows in Park Lane, between Mayfair and High Park, opened in 2006 with a dazzling view on the twenty-eighth floor of the Park Lane Hilton. Named for chef Chris Galvin, the restaurant specializes in rich, haute cuisine French food with Asian and British influence. Lunch entrees start at £25. For details or to make reservations call 020 7208 4021, or click on: www.galvinatwindows.com

Located in the Mayfair district just across from St. George's Hanover Square, Wild Honey is a tiny gem. Notable dishes include unique seasonal food like the delicious rabbit pork and apricot terrine. There is an extensive wine list. Three-course lunches are £21.95; pre-theatre three course meals are £22.95. For more information or to make a reservation, call 020 7758 9160, or click on: www.wildhoneyrestaurant.co.uk

Kensington Place is a large, airy restaurant at the top of Kensington Church Street. It specializes in fresh seafood with a Mediterranean flair. Located in the same Notting Hill location for the past quarter century, Kensington Place was renovated in 2011 and got a new menu which focused on fresh fish and seafood. The owners have a fish shop right next door. For information, call 020 7727 3184, or click on: www.kensingtonplace-restaurant.co.uk

Be our guest at Dinner by Heston Blumenthal. Located At the Mandarin Oriental, this bright uplifting restaurant reinvented dishes like eighteenth-century Salamugundy (chicken, salsify, marrow bone) and

Taffety Tart (apple, rose, fennel and blackcurrant sorbet). This is worth a try for the unusual and delectable food and the views over Hyde Park. For more information and to see a menu, call: 020 7201 3833, or click on: www.dinnerbyheston.com

If you can find Simpson's Tavern then you deserve to eat there. It's like a treasure hunt. South of Bank, on Ball Court at 38 Cornhill, the tavern is actually two seventeenth-century houses. Note the bottle-bottom glass windows. Simpson's promises "Good honest fare" is served in old-fashioned stalls. Dine in the Grill Room or the restaurant proper. Simpson's pub fare includes pies, puddings and English cheeseboards. For details call 020 7626 9985, or click on: www.simpsonstavern.co.uk

Located on Trafalgar Square in the old St. Martin's eighteenth century converted crypt, Café in the Crypt is worth dining there for the cocktail conversation material alone. However, it is also a great deal: Sunday lunch for £7.95. In the heart of London, Café in the Crypt serves cafeteria-style meals in gallery café style. Dishes include hearty English food, proper teas, generous breakfasts and attractive soup-and-a-roll options. Wednesday night is jazz nights. Call 020 7766 1158, or click on: www.smitf.org. Be sure you get photos and post to your Facebook friends that you ate in a crypt!

Coq d'Argent is located at 1 Poultry atop James Stirling's pink and terracotta building. The rooftop restaurant, bar and brasserie serves classic French food that befits its name, during the week. Weekends are reserved for jazz and brunch. The £28 Sunday Jazz lunch is memorable. For details or reservations call 020 7395 5000, or click on: www.coqdargent.co.uk

Morito is a tapas bar located right beside Moro in Exmouth Market. Most of the delectable bites cost under £8. Men would find this spot not filling enough but women love the portions and the variety. Morito takes lunchtime reservations but dinner—served Monday through Saturday—is on a first come first served basis. For details or reservations, call 020 7278 7007, www.moro.co.uk

Northbank at the Millennium Bridge offers a view of the city side of the river. Located on the Thames Path looking up at the Wobbly Bridge, Northbank offers good food and a kick-ass view. The menu is simple, modern British food for a good price. Children under twelve eat free on Saturdays, for example. Ask to be seated outside on the terrace with views across at Tate Modern. For details or to make reservations, call 020 7329 9299, or click on: www.northbankrestaurant.com

The London Art Scene

No matter what your specific interest in art is, you will find a wealth of art galleries, art studios, street art and performance art to satisfy your cravings.

Tate Britain is the British national gallery of art, which dates from 1500 to the present day. It is a ten-minute walk from Westminster Abbey and faces the river. Tate Britain holds British art by Blake, Hodgkin Epstein, Gainsborough, Constable, Sickert, Gilbert and George, Hatoum, Hockney, Stubbs, Hogarth, Moore, Hirst, Rossetti, Spencer, and Turner. For more information click on:http://www.tate.org.uk/visit/tate-britain

Tate Modern houses art from the 1900s to today. Located on the Southbank, in the former Bankside Power Station Tate Modern is Britain's national gallery of international modern art including works by Dalí, Matisse, Picasso, Rothko and Warhol as well as contemporary work by artists such as Dorothy Cross, Susan Hiller and Gilbert & George. The gallery is beside the Globe Theatre opposite St Paul's Cathedral, which is connected by a footbridge across the River Thames. For information on exhibits and special events click on: http://shop.tate.org.uk/shop/exhibitions/icat/exhibitions

Located on the north side of Trafalgar Square, the National Gallery houses a collection masterpieces that trace the development of Western European painting. Eighteen rooms house priceless paintings from Leonardo Da Vinci to Vincent Van Gogh. The National Gallery, London, houses one of the greatest collections of European painting in the world-over 2000 European paintings dating from the thirteenth century to 1900 in a landmark building. Take the virtual tour at: http://www.nationalgallery.org.uk/virtualtour#/central-hall/

For more information and hours of operation, click on: http://www.nationalgallery.org.uk/. Admission is free 361 days of the year.

Next door is the Portrait Gallery. Founded in 1856, it contains a collection of portraits of famous British men and women. The 120,000 portraits date from the 16th Century to the present day.

The British Museum located in the Bloomsbury, houses an extensive collection of art works including jewellery, coins. The collection is dedicated to the history art and culture of mankind. The museum is open daily and admission is free. For more information click on: http://www.britishmuseum.org/

The Wallace Collection, located in the Oxford Street shopping district, has unequalled displays of French eighteenth century painting, furniture and porcelain with superb Old Master paintings. The Wallace Collection is housed in an historic London town house. Its Twenty-five galleries are unsurpassed in their collections, private possessions of eighteenth and nineteenth centuries first four Marquesses of Hertford and Sir Richard Wallace. For details click on: http://www.wallacecollection.org/

The Saatchi Gallery is located at The Duke of York's HQ, in King's Road. It is open seven days a week and admission is free to all exhibits. The building is 70,000 square feet and can accommodate large contemporary works the private permanent collection of the Saatchi brothers. The current exhibits are the work of modern artists from Africa and Latin America. For more information click on: http://www.saatchigallery.com/

The Serpentine Collection is a little-known gallery in Kensington Gardens. It showcases modern and contemporary art by the finest contemporary artists working in a wide variety of media. The Gallery harbors a permanent work by poet and artist Ian Hamilton Finlay, dedicated to the Patrointernational modern artn of Serpentine, Diana, Princess of Wales. For more information click on: http://www.serpentinegalleries.org/

In addition to art exhibits London hosts many art shows at various locations throughout the city. Whitehall Gallery currently has an exhibition that takes off after Tate Modern. It is called "Adventures of the Black Square" and is a modern abstract art show featuring art from 1915 to 2015.

The Tate Sensorium challenges visitors to appreciate art not just visually but with their other senses as well. Beginning in September the British Museum will have an exhibit of Celtic art.

London's best street art is located in the heart of Shoreditch, in London's East End. Shoreditch is an area that requires investigation. It is home to a vibrant and colourful culture of street art, murals, cafes, bars, galleries, restaurants, fashion and markets. Street artists from London's east end and all over Europe have left their mark in beautiful, unusual and energetic creations on the walls of Shoreditch. Street art is constantly shifting in style and location. New work is being created by new artists who come to the area. Yesterday's masterpieces are today's new canvasses.

Take a self-guided or guided walk and enjoy some of the amazing works like Puerto Rican artists Juan Fernandez and Alexis Diaz murals. Both artists paint fantastically detailed murals depicting animal imagery. Alexis Diaz's best known London piece was the elephant-octopus mural located along Hanbury Street. Composed of tiny brushstrokes, it took him a full week to paint.

Banksy has established himself as one of the most renowned contemporary artists. Banksy's street work in the 2000's defined the whole genre of street art. One of his 2002 works is located on Old Street.

Colombian street artist Bastardilla is famous for her sparkling street art. She often uses glitter into her pieces. Her tag is a tiny hummingbird, which she leaves on her works.

Street artist Ben Wilson painstakingly paints on discarded chewing gum. His technique involves super-heating the gum with a blow torch, spraying it with lacquer, applying enamel and then creating a tiny image with miniature paint brushes before sealing the gum with a layer of clear lacquer. He has painted thousands of pieces of gum around London. You will find many pieces along the Millennium Bridge across the Thames and on Muswell Hill where he lives.

Some galleries have begun to exhibit this street art or graffiti. One of these is Graffiti Life now run by Proof. It is an independent gallery on London's East End in the heart of London's Street Art scene. The gallery holds regular shows focusing on works from artists that actively participate in the culture of Graffiti in a wide variety works, across all media. For more information on the current graffiti art exhibits click on: http://thegraffitilifegallery.co.uk/

Another amazing and unorthodox art form that abounds in London is performance art.

Street performers are often found in the Covent Garden area. They must audition for spots to perform there and must be licensed. Covent Garden is famous clowns, acrobats, magicians, and fire-eaters who situate themselves between the piazza and St. Paul's Church. A perfect spot to watch them is from the balcony of the Punch and Judy Pub.

The basement of the Piazza usually has opera singers and classical musicians. You can sit at one of the cafes in the basement level and enjoy coffee while listening to the music.

Another favourite Southbank location is between The London Eye and Tate Modern. Enjoy a leisurely walk along the Southbank stopping to watch street performers. These people make a living or supplement their income by doing street performances. These might include acrobats, mime, and magic tricks.

Shopping in London

No trip to London England would be complete without exploring London's varied and exciting shopping options.

London has many distinct retail areas and shopping streets. Quite a few of them have unique themes and specialties. You could spend a week in each area exploring and window shopping. In order to help you direct your shopping days to the areas in which you are most interested, let's consider some of the most distinctive areas.

If you are looking for luxury goods then head over to [Mayfair](). The Bond Street and Mayfair area is a wonderful place to window shop even if you don't have the money for the top designer clothes. You can also people watch those celebrities on a shopping spree. The Mayfair shopping area is home to famous names like: [Burberry](), [Louis Vuitton]() and [Tiffany & Co](). South Molton Street is worth a stroll to browse at Browns' iconic fashion store, Browns. The famous Mayfair shopping area is easily reached from Tube stops at Piccadilly Circus and Bond Street.

If it is quirky treasures you are seeking, you are most likely to find these in Covent Garden. Accessed by the Covent Garden or Leicester Square Tube stations, this area is just brimming with hip fashion, unique gifts, rare sweet treats or unique, handmade jewellery. Covent Garden is worth the time just to look at the goods and people watch. Neal Street is the home of urban streetwear, funky cosmetics and shoes. Take some time to explore the unusual Neal's Garden. Be sure to check out the original arts and crafts on Monmouth Street, Floral Street, Shorts Gardens, St Martin's Courtyard, and Seven Dials. Covent Garden area is London's famously distinctive treasure shopping area.

If you crave large shopping centres Westfield is a good choice. Westfield has two magnificent shopping malls in London located at White City and Stratford. Westfield London has favourite British shops: Debenhams, Next, Marks & Spencer and House of Fraser. Westfield also hosts luxury brands like: Louis Vuitton, Jimmy Choo, All Saints and Ted Baker.

While you are at Westfield, you might want to take a break from shopping to go to the cinema, the gym, slip into one of the several bars and restaurants for a cocktail or dinner.

Westfield Stratford City in East London has 250 shops and 70 places to eat. It's the largest shopping mall in Europe—all under one roof!

The nearest Tube station for Westfield London is White City or Shepherds Bush. The Stratford stop provides access to Westfield Stratford City.

King's Road is just off the Sloane Square Tube stop. It offers an eclectic mix of unique labels, trendy boutiques, high-street staples and designer shops. Take some time to stroll and stop at one of the many cafes and exclusive eateries. King's Road is home to such interior designers as Peter Jones, Heal's and Cath Kidston. Take a trip back in time to where seventies fashion was born, at Vivienne Westwood's shop, or go antiquing at Chelsea Antiques Market.

Oxford Street is a shopper's haven with over three hundred shops and stores. It is located in the heart of London shopping. This bustling, exciting street has everything from small shops to designer outlets and landmark stores. On Oxford Street you will find Selfridges. It is also home to famous department stores like: John Lewis and Debenhams. For small independent and one-of-a-kind stores choose one of Oxford's side streets, such as St Christopher's Place and Berwick Street. Oxford Street shopping is conveniently located near the Tube stops at: Oxford Circus, Bond Street or Tottenham Court Road.

Just a few blocks away is the famous sixties fashion area Carnaby Street. Carnaby and its thirteen surrounding streets are just two minutes away from Tube stations at Oxford Circus and Circus. The Carnaby Street area is worth a stroll for 150 shopping and over 50 dining options. Carnaby Street shopping area offers intriguing stores, independent boutiques, heritage brands, and new designer names.

Take a shopping break at one of the many restaurants, bars, cafés and great English pubs including Kingly Court, just off Carnaby Street.

Savile Row known as "the golden mile off tailoring" has long held a reputation for fine craftsmanship and custom tailored clothes. Convenient to Piccadilly Circus and Bond Street Tube stations, Savile Row is worth a stroll to see Henry Poole & Co, the first Savile Row tailor and inventor of the tuxedo. Other iconic names in British tailoring include Gieves & Hawkes, Huntsman & Sons, and Ozwald Boateng. The corner is home of the flagship Abercrombie & Fitch store.

The movie "Notting Hill" put this area on every shopper's bucket list. Accessed by Tube Stations at Notting Hill, Ladbroke Grove and Westbourne Park, Notting Hill offers the adventurous shopping hundreds of small shops selling vintage clothing, rare antiques, unusual gifts, books and organic food. Take time to explore the mile-long [Portobello Road Market](#)'s interesting stalls. There's something new set out daily. Westbourne Grove, nearby, has high-end shopping; designer shops as well as quirky boho boutiques, chic cafes and art galleries. It's worth the shopping experience just to say you were actually where the movie was made!

To explore a unique area of London get off at the Canary Wharf Tube stop. This is London's Docklands area. It is also home to many of Britain's leading businesses. Finally, and most important to shoppers, Canary Wharf is home to Canada Square, a sleek, modern shopping centre containing over two hundred shops. Included are famous makes like Oasis, Zaram Myla lingerie shop and Jo Malone famous fragrances.

If you want to experience a "pop up" mall, get off the Tube at Old Street or Liverpool Street. In East London, Shoreditch is home to CEO Roger Wade's mall opened in 2011. The mall will be open for only four years. It was built, so it could be deconstructed. Its materials are stripped and refitted shipping containers. Aptly named Boxpark, this unique pop up mall includes fashion and lifestyle brands, galleries, cafés and restaurants.

London Walking and Biking Tours

London is a great place to see on foot because of its many distinctive neighbourhoods. You can get out a map and set your sites on wandering the various sections of London. You can enjoy the various cultures of London by using the shopping districts as walking tours. You can acquire maps and tour books that outline London tours. You can get an audio tour of London to accompany your walk. Or you can take a guided tour where a knowledgeable local will point out things you would have missed. There are advantages and disadvantages to each plan for walking about this city.

Guided walking tours are available all year round in London. For many, you can just turn up, pay the tour guide and join in. There are themed tours, which may have great appeal because of your special interests or goals. You might like to take a special trail. For example: The London Heart Trail runs between the [London Eye](#) and [City Hall](#) along London's picturesque South Bank. It is a free walking trail designed to encourage visitors to see London and get healthier while doing so. You can download an app for this trail from iTunes or the Apple Store.

If you are into bridges you can walk the waterfront area and see a good many of them. This self-guided tour follows parts of the Thames Path and takes you along the river front where it is accessible. Start at the Westminster Tube Station then Exit opposite Big Ben and turn left towards the river. Cross Westminster Bridge and turn left towards London Eye, along the riverfront. For details click on: http://www.londonforfree.net/walks/bridges-walk/

If you want to see up close the many iconic attractions that bring people to London you can do this with a self-guided tour that includes: Big Ben, the Houses of Parliament, St. Margaret's Church, The Jewel Tower, Dean's Yard, Westminster School, Westminster Abbey The Prime Minister's residence, The Horse Guards, the cenotaph, and more. https://www.londontoolkit.com/walks/whitehall_walk_westminster.htm

The City of London Tour takes in The Tower of London. It is a circle tour so you can start at a spot that is most convenient for you. A good part of the self-guided walking tour is within the old City of London, when it had a city wall. Ghost walk commercial tours take place here on weekend so it is a good idea—if you want to avoid crowds—to do this one on a weekday. https://www.londontoolkit.com/walks/pool_london_walk_tower_london.htm

The Kensington area walk is only two miles but there are so many interesting things to see and do that it will likely take lots longer. The Portobello Market alone is worth hours of browsing. For details of this area commemorating Princess Diana's life, click on: https://www.londontoolkit.com/walks/kensington_walk_north.htm The walk includes Kensington Palace, The Round Pond, and Diana, Princess of Wales Memorial Playground.

Biking in and around London

Several companies offer bike rentals and/or guided bike tours of London. One of them is the London Bicycle Tour Company located at Gabriel's Wharf, 56 Upper Ground, London SE1 9PP, United Kingdom. They offer six different guided tours as well as bicycle rentals and bike repairs. For information on their tours and prices click on: http://www.londonbicycle.com/

You can also choose to be creative and see the city from other modes of transportation. See London by moped. Click on: www.londonbikeandscooter.co.uk

Or http://www.google.ca/search?hl=en&q=scooter+hire+london&btnG=Google+Search&meta=

Imagine riding through one of London's spacious parks on horseback. Several riding stables offer riding lessons, guided horseback tours and horse rental for unguided tours. See London via horse trails: http://www.hydeparkstables.com/

See London by helicopter: https://www.thelondonhelicopter.com/

When you are contemplating seeing London, why not include an aerial view? Rise up above the sights and sounds of London and fly away in a quiet, hot air balloon. Flights are about an hour. After the flight the balloon crew will return you to a nearby Underground or Rail station so you can return to you London accommodations. The whole hot air balloon experience takes four to six hours so be sure to allow enough time. Flights can occur only on weekdays and only in calm, clear weather for both safety and visibility. For more information on how to see London from a hot air balloon, click on: https://www.adventureballoons.co.uk/london-balloon-flights

Before you leave London, take a ride on a double decker bus.

Like the San Francisco trams and the Branson Missouri ducks, the double decker buses are a great way to see London. The buses, which have been in operation for sixty years, make over eighty conveniently located stops across London affording sightseers innumerable photo opportunities. You can buy a twenty-four-hour ticket and hop on and off at will. When you see something you want to examine in depth or a building you want to tour, you just pop off at that stop and get back on one of the regularly scheduled buses when you are ready to move on to your next tourist attraction. The double decker buses stop at all London's famous landmarks.

Your twenty-four-hour-ticket also includes a cruise on the Thames. On the cruise you will get a chance to see London from a different perspective while you sail along the River Thames. Board the boat at either Westminster Pier, close by the Houses of Parliament, or at Tower Pier, at the Tower of London. The cruise gives a great view of Shakespeare's Globe Theatre, South Bank, and the London Eye. Your twenty-four-hour-original-tours-ticket lets you board both the bus and the boat as many times as you want within twenty-four hours. If you didn't get to see all of London you wanted to explore within one day, you can upgrade to a forty-eight-hour ticket. For more information, click on: https://www.theoriginaltour.com/

Conclusion

London—unlike many European cities—is modern and fast-paced. It is an energetic international centre of business, finance and arts and culture. Travelling alone or as part of a group, tourists need to be able to travel about the city by foot, bicycle, cab, bus and/or Tube. As in any other large city, try to avoid travel during rush hour. It makes your trip less stressful as you set out to use an unfamiliar metro system if you do not have to deal with crowds too. Give yourself lots of time to get where you are going. Taxis can get stuck in traffic. Buses can run late. The Tube may be overcrowded. London is not a place where you want to be rushed. Savour your experience and don't try to pack everything into a day.

I guarantee you, like the millions who visit London each year, will want to return to do the things you didn't get around to on this visit.

Count on eating a big breakfast. It's part of the culture but it is also a smart move. Food and eating out are expensive in the UK compare to North America. Many accommodations come with full breakfast included so you will save money and time if you take advantage of this meal. It will also sustain you for the walking you are sure to want to do as you sightsee and shop and get to know the many London neighbourhoods.

Think about day trips outside London. If this is your first trip to the city you may not wish to venture outside the city but future trips offer that option. Two great day trips are to Cambridge and Bath. Cambridge is a lovely college town. Walk around the grounds of the colleges. Try punting down the River Camden.

Bath is unique, part Roman excavation and part Victorian. Tour the Roman baths. They are surprisingly intact. Stroll down Pulteney Bridge and browse through the stores that are located on the bridge itself.

Before you buy things remember the conversion. While the amounts LOOK similar to North American dollars remember they are in pounds and thus two to three times as much. Yes, things are expensive. So, if you are buying something remember what you are really paying for it. Then if you really want it, buy it anyway.

Also check out coupons and other savings. A good sight is: http://www.smartsave.com/uk/ gives you discount vouchers for pretty much everything. You can pick up 20% off vouchers for all the main attractions and it's all free!

Eat where the locals eat. It's a more interesting experience and a lot cheaper. You will find that pub food is tasty, substantial and authentic. Besides, this will give you a golden opportunity to talk to the locals and maybe even get invited to share a game of darts.

If you are on a tight budget there are lots of London sights like museums, parks, street performers, galleries, and walking tours that are absolutely free. Check out reasonable accommodations at places like youth hostels and these inexpensive London digs at: http://www.theguardian.com/travel/2011/may/06/top-10-budget-hotels-london

Travel in and around London is very easy once you get the hang of it. The Tube, trains and buses and even the double decker original tour day pass is much more reasonable than taking cabs or limos. London is also a city that lends itself to walking. However, safety trumps expense. If you are going out after traveling in groups then take safe transportation.

Helpful Resources

Newman, K. (2014) What I Was Doing While You Were Breeding. http://www.amazon.ca/What-Doing-While-Were-Breeding/dp/0804137609

Ross, A. "Why Every Woman Should Travel Alone". http://time.com/3708374/women-travel-alone/

Women Traveling Together. https://www.women-traveling.com/

PREVIEW OTHER BOOKS BY THIS AUTHOR

"FLORENCE FOR WOMEN: THE ULTIMATE TRAVEL GUIDE FOR WOMEN"

by Erica Stewart

[Excerpt from the first 2 Chapters – for complete book, please purchase on Amazon.com]

History and Culture

Any Florence travel guide can never be complete without detailing its rich history and culture. Our guide might specifically cater to our female readers, but it's still important to understand the area's history and culture, isn't it?

The history of Florence can be traced all the way back to the Etruscan times. The city was then known as Fiesole, one that dominated the entire region and was one of the most important Etruscan centers. As the Romans prepared for their war against Fiesole, they set up camp by the Arno River in the 1st century BC. This area was later called Florentia, which can roughly be translated to "destined to flower". Florence somehow managed to survive the Middle Ages as well, and soon became one of the most important cities on the planet.

Florence's growth suffered a major setback because of a dispute between the Ghibellines, those loyal to Emperor Frederick II, and the Guelfs, those loyal to the pope. This led to the Guelfs being exiled from the city, but their absence was apparently short-lived, for they took over Florence once the Emperor succumbed to his death. Despite all the political turmoil, great attention was paid to arts and architecture, and this is one of the main reasons why Florence stands like a shining architectural jewel and a stark reminder of the romantic architectural wonders of a bygone era.

Art and culture were integral to the way of life as well. The desire of its locals to educate themselves led to the birth of the first works in the vernacular language in the form of "Dolce stil novo". This later inspired countless artists such as Boccaccio, Dante and Petrarch as well. In fact, Boccaccio's documentation of the Florence plague is one of the most accurate descriptions of a tragedy that began as dissatisfaction and ended with the "Tumulto dei Ciompi" in the year 1378.

Florence saw a small period where the people took over the rule of the city. However, this was evidently short-lived as the Medici dynasty soon took over. The Medici emperor Lorenzo il Magnifico was also responsible for much of the city's wonderful Brunelleschi architecture. After his death in the year 1492, the city once again fell into turmoil, but this era of conflict still managed to see the rise of world famous artists such as Leonardo da Vinci and Michelangelo.

From the 18th century up until the very beginning of the 20th century, Florence remained famous for its literary offerings and artistic wonders. It produced some of the best works of literature created by writers such as Palazzeschi, Papini and Pratolini, all of whom were members of the literary group "Giubbe Rosse".

Getting There and Around

Florence is well connected to the rest of Europe and is easy to get into. It has witnessed a drastic increase in tourism over the past few years, and this has led to the development of all sorts of high-tech facilities and traveler-friendly infrastructure.

Getting There

The best way to travel to Florence is by air. The Aeroporto Firenze-Peretola is the main airport of Florence and is located at a distance of 2.5 miles from the city center. The ideal way to commute from the airport is to board the shuttle bus, which connects the airport to the Santa Maria Novella station and runs at intervals of 30 minutes between 06.00AM and 11.40PM. Taxi services are available as well.

Getting Around

It makes sense to leave your cars behind while traveling to Florence. And even if you're coming from a faraway destination, forget all about that car rental. As women, one of our main concerns is our security, particularly when traveling to different countries. However, when it comes to Florence, you really don't need a car for most of its major attractions are located in its historic city center, an area best explored on foot (vehicles aren't allowed to enter the city center without prior authorization either). And visiting other destinations is easy as well, for Florence boasts of a decent public transportation system that lets you get from point A to point B without much fuss.

I recommend using the taxi services while in the city, particularly if you're traveling alone. Florence taxis are white in color and can be picked up from a taxi rank or be booked on the phone. Taxi ranks can easily be found in front of the main plazas and railway stations. Some of the top taxi operators in Florence include SO.CO.TA (+39 055 4242) and CO.TA.FI (+39 055 4390).

Florence is relatively small, and this means that a woman can really have a blast while exploring its streets on a bike. There are a number of cycle tracks in the city as well, and this certainly makes things easier. Some of the top bike rental companies to hire your bikes from include Alinari (+39 055 280500), Rentway (+333 9619820), and Florence by bike (+39 055 488992).

For women who like to keep it adventurous, the Segway offers a fascinating option of getting from one place to the other. It's convenient, it's simple and it's certainly super exciting. You can book your Segways by calling +39 055 2398855.

Finally, it is very hard to resist the romantic feel of riding in an open carriage. These enchanting rides transport you to a bygone era and Florence's enchanting cobblestone streets offer the perfect backdrop to relive yesterday. You can easily pick up a carriage in Piazza San Giovanni, Piazza Duomo & Piazza della Signoria.

Staying in Florence

Florence is one of the top cities in Italy for any woman wanting to choose from a wide range of safe, secure, exciting and inviting accommodations. Florence was among the first cities in Italy to develop its hotel scene, particularly because of the efforts of local designer Michele Bonan, who has now left his mark on hotels across the country, and the hospitality division of the Ferragamo Group, Lungarno Hotels.

Hotels for Every Budget

The city has always enjoyed a great tradition of hospitality and she takes a lot of pride in introducing her female travelers to some of its best-kept secrets. There's a lot of choice across all budgets, even in the historic city center, the place where you really want to be. Better yet, the competition amongst hotels keeps rates at a low, particularly during the off season.

For Ladies Wanting to Live like Locals

If you're dreaming of staying in an area that is full of artisan workshops, real people and hidden cafes, look no further than the Oltrarno district. Some of the top accommodation options include the cute B&B Floroom 1 and the Palazzo Magnani Feroni.

Billed as one of the top bed and breakfasts in the city, **B&B Floroom 1** is a sleek address located on the banks of the Arno River, and one of the top choices for solo female travelers looking for budgeted options in the city. This four-bedroom B&B boasts of an extremely relaxed atmosphere and each of its four rooms feature wooden floors, white walls, rustic ceilings and giant photographs of Florence. The old-new combination works quite well and really makes the property stand out. Some rooms also boast of four-poster beds, and an opaque glass wall hides away the comfy bathroom that has been fitted with pewter fittings and rainforest showerheads.

The **Palazzo Magnani Feroni** is one hotel that you'd never want to leave. It makes you feel like the nobility of yesterday and transports you to a historic location that makes you forget about everything else. Each aristocratic suite boasts of beautiful high curved ceilings and heirloom furniture and the terrace views rank among the very best.

For the Budget-Conscious Woman (Medium Range)
Casa Di Barbano is a simple option that offers great value for money. It is spacious and elegant and its owners are extremely friendly. All rooms are comfortable to say the least, and when you factor in the convenient location, safe accommodations, and

reasonable costs, you have everything you need to explore Florence like a pro.

Casa Nuestra is one of the hippest addresses in the city. This brand new B&B is located close to the Campo di Marte station, and is characterized by its super friendly hosts. Apart from offering picture-perfect accommodations, the owners also go out of their way to assist you in planning your itineraries, show you how to explore the city and help you uncover enchanting walking paths.

For the Lady Who Travels in Style…. (Luxury)

Palazzo Vecchietti is one of the most elegant and beautiful hotels in the city. This boutique hotel boasts of stylish rooms, easy access to Via Tornabuoni and a superior level of service. The furnishings have been tastefully appointed, and great attention has been paid to every detail. Beds are comfy and usually include quality beddings and cashmere blankets. They are the just about the perfect places to snuggle into after a long and tiring day exploring the artistic wonders around the city.

Another popular option is the **St. Regis Hotel**. It boasts of a unique ambience that is both delightful and discreet at the same time. The hotel is located on an enchanting riverside location in centro storico and its Arno views appeals to female travelers who are accustomed to the highest standards of pampering. The service is warm and welcoming, professional and casual, discreet and attentive. Everything you'd want it to be. And the rooms are just what you'd expect from a hotel like St. Regis. I would recommend the Bottega Veneta suite, a top option for fashion-conscious women.

Things to See and Do

No matter how many times you come to visit this iconic beauty, you won't be able to see it all. A bridge on the Arno River is one of the first destinations that you should visit while in Florence. It is known to offer different experiences at different times of the day, for the views, the light, and the atmosphere changes each and every time. Considered to be the birthplace of the Renaissance, Florence also boasts of some of the best art and architecture in history. No wonder it manages to draw millions of tourists year after year.

Walking in the Footsteps of Michelangelo

Very few artists have managed to leave their mark on a city the way Michelangelo has in Florence. The city is home to some of his greatest masterpieces, and one of the biggest charms of visiting the city is to retrace his steps and explore places that are linked to his memories. Embarking on the following itinerary not only lets you retrace Michelangelo's steps, but also brings you closer to some of the most important arts and monuments in Florence. Remember, the ideal way to make the most of this itinerary is to spread it over two days, so that you get enough time to marvel at the various wonders and enjoy all that it has in store for you.

Start off your explorations at the **Casa Buonarroti**. Located in the vibrant Santa Croce, Casa Buonarroti is the palace where the artist's family lived. It was built by his nephew Leonardo, and passed hands from one member of the family to another until the iconic family finally became extinct. Casa Buonarroti hosts some of the earliest works of Michelangelo such as the *Madonna della Scala* and the *Battle of the Centaurs*. The former is a tribute to sculptor Donatello while the latter has been inspired by the Garden of San Marco. Both masterpieces were created by the artist while he was in his twenties, and imagining a young boy creating such outstanding works of art is an exciting experience in itself.

The next destination is the **Church of Santo Spirito**, another place that has been intricately linked with Michelangelo during his early days. Located in the Oltrarno district, the church is considered to be one of the most beautiful Renaissance-era churches on the planet. It was also the place where Michelangelo found accommodation after his patron Lorenzo de Medici died in the year 1492. The church is famous for its inspiring wooden *Crucifix* that Michelangelo created in the year 1493.

The next step of your journey takes you to the **Bargello Museum**. Michelangelo was forced to move to Rome in the year 1494 after the city riots sent Medici into exile, and it was in Rome that he created the world famous *Bacchus*, now located in the Bargello Museum. The museum is also home to other popular artworks created by the artist such as *David/ Apollo, Brutus,* and *Tondo Pitti*.

Don't forget to add the **Accademia Gallery** into your itinerary as well. Once Michelangelo returned to Florence in the year 1501, he set about creating some of his best works of art, including the outstanding *David*, now located in the Accademia Gallery. The Accademia is also home to many of his unfinished figures and sculptures. From the *"non finito"* sculpting techniques of *St. Matthew* to the marble wonder *Prigioni*, the Accademia truly showcases some of the most the distinct features of Michelangelo's style.

Head over to the **Uffizi Art Gallery** next. Considered to be one of the most famous art galleries in the world, Uffizi features a large collection of artworks created between the 12th and 17th centuries by leading artists such as Leonardo da Vinci, Botticelli, Raffaello and Giotto. The gallery also houses the *Tondo Doni*, Michelangelo's first canvas painting and the only of its kind in Florence.

Between the years 1515 and 1534, the Medici family saw two of its members becoming popes – Clement VII and Leo X. Michelangelo was commissioned to create the *Laurentian Library* for the *Basilica of San Lorenzo* and the *Sagrestia Nuova* for the **Medici Chapels**. Both works of art are a must see and the entire complex is also worth a visit for its artistic ingenuity.

The last Michelangelo masterpiece that you should admire during your stay in Florence is the *Pieta Bandini*. This dramatic work of art was created in the year 1550 and is now located in the **Museo dell'Opera del Duomo**. It is considered to be one of the greatest examples of the master's work and what makes it even more special is his self-portrait, a male figure flanked by Mary and Magdalene, holding the lifeless body of Christ.

Best Neighborhoods

When planning any vacation, one of the biggest concerns for women is to choose the right neighborhood. There are some areas that have traditionally been famous for being safe for women, while ensuring that they don't miss out on the very best of nightlife and cosmopolitan delights that the city has to offer. When it comes to Florence, you need to decide between three choices – staying in the historic center, staying outside of the historic center or staying in the surrounding countryside. All three areas have safe neighborhoods for women, so it ultimately boils down to personal preference. Here are a few options to choose from.

Staying Within the Historic Center

The city center always dominates a major part of your holiday for most of the historic sights and attractions are located here. The area is among the oldest parts of the city, and the ring that you see is basically the spot where those 13th century walls were built. The city center is quite small, and car free as well. This means that you can easily walk from one place to the other and not miss a car throughout your journey. Staying close to the Santa Maria Novella station puts you within a 5-minute walk from the Duomo and staying close to the Duomo puts you within a 5-minute walk from Ponte Vecchio and Palazzo Vecchio. The ideal way to choose an area is to look for accommodations close to the sites you really like. Since most of the major sites are quite close to each other, I suggest staying between Piazza Santa Croce, Piazza San Marco, Piazza Santa Maria Novella and Ponte Vecchio. This area is among the busiest areas in the city and is always full of tourists all through the day and in the evenings as well. The second option is to look for accommodations in the Oltrarno neighborhood, but that only works if you're leaning towards local experiences, unique furniture galleries and the Pitti Palace.

Staying Outside the Historic Center

With most of the restaurants, cafes, sights and attractions located within the historic center, you would argue if it makes sense to stay outside the center. However, many female travelers visiting Florence end up booking accommodations outside its historic center for all sorts of reasons. The biggest advantage of staying outside the city center is that it is friendlier on the wallet. Moreover, anyone wanting to stay in a residential area to explore the local way of life needs to step outside the touristic city center. A few areas that aren't really far from the main sights of the city include Via Bolognese, Fortezza da Basso, Poggio Imperiale and Piazza Beccaria.

Staying in the Surrounding Countryside

If you're thinking of keeping Florence as a base for exploring Tuscany, you might want to head over to the surrounding hills. Apart from letting you get up close and personal to nature, it also lets you enjoy all sorts of amenities such as gardens, outdoor areas and swimming pools in your accommodations without forcing you to pay through the roof. Having your own rental car is a must while staying in the outskirts, but it's perfect for exploring Tuscany to its fullest.

[Excerpt from the first 2 Chapters – for complete book, please purchase on Amazon.com]

Made in the USA
Coppell, TX
09 February 2022